introduction.

I used to twist your locs on Sunday afternoons

then you left.

i found myself the
l
k
  n
    o
     t
   t
e
 d

alone and dreaded.

I have the task of introducing *ndgo* to you, the reader. I have the burden of explaining what this project means in terms of love and living, of experiencing and engaging. It intimidates me - attempting to discuss what this book is and why it means as much as it does. My intimidation comes at no unnecessary hesitation; community based projects rely heavily on the community to accept them and without their acceptance, projects like these are worth nothing. Instead of trying to explain *this* particular project, I want to talk about why this book and similar creations are necessary to the survival of Our art and Our experiences as human beings capable of love, sadness, happiness and reflection among an even greater variety of feelings.

My good friend and companion Spook has written the following pages with the heart in mind. Spook's task is a feat - the heart rarely travels intentionally to the mind but routinely overrides the brain with commands to which only it knows the code. We met four or five years ago in Washington, D.C. where we were first beginning to understand what it meant to be ourselves and the power of those embodiments. I found Spook had been working for some time on her life as a compilation of art, soul and love. I fell into sync with the rhythm of her dissonance. Since that first meeting, I have witnessed in Spook a relentless energy to find the truth in her circumstances, whether ugly or pretty. That pursuit of truth, at all costs, has developed into a science of intellectual analysis through the lens of the human experience. In some ways, she looks to merge the heart and the mind into one complete program, an equation with a reasonable solution, a flower with its own distinct scent.

The manifestation of this project should be a signal to whomever is reading that your possibilities are just as real. By no small coincidence, we are imprinted on these pages that your being is able to conceive. We thank you for sharing your warmth with us. We truly believe that one fire can light many torches, one Love can transform all. Thank you for lighting up with us.

-CTTN

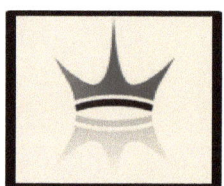

many thanks to those who came before…even if they did not stay.
-spook.

Neo Ego Trip.

((i am the contemporary of your
repentance for past loves lost.))

--a stark reminder and the
solution to your Prison of ills.

i am exactly what god made.
--and sometimes a bit less,
but never shy of being
crafted of the earth
in the shape of heaven--

a vessel of the voice
of creation.
i create because i was created.
and created to create-
hardly ever engaging in recreation
i re-create.

realizing the value in hard work…
in the sweetness of shit
turned to sugar.

16.

did you know you rocked me?
--no more blues over you::
just sunshine.
--at a memory's thought...
remember?
...the time...
bout 7a.m. i said
good morning to heartache--
met you blue and green at
dawn--
jill say what's new?

--feeling like an uneasy sunday--
with thunder, but absent of rain--
tell me how to become the love
you initiated
in this space...
//

black rose.

she goes//
where most would never--
to the places where the Dirtiest
take habitat...
//she knows//
the Beauty of roses
reaching thru concrete--

and she has felt the pain of gravel
against the softness of her petals...
crooked little
insecure flower--
held up by the
floor of the jungle...

walked over
stepped on--
and still.

17.

he had told me
about the women he loved//
never up close
but pinned to the walls of his apartment://
and how they never spoke back
but always gave the answer--

and the Truth lies somewhere
between the top and bottom of a Woman's
curve.

--so he kept them far far…
only images to
explore
and Create with…
his hurt causing his hearts
immunity to
the Closeness of
Emotion.

18.

i've outgrown the chase of you...
have to maintain focus--

...and if my fingertips are on your
back,
...it won't be because you slipped
out my hands--

//i won't say i'll wait either--
...because these poems keep going
as musings pass by...
i wouldn't not write a word.

On & On[er]

like one two three.
oh what a day.

colder in my summer.
hotter in my fall.

lets--
fall
...

into the puddle of god...

like the raindrops we are...

on & on...

evaporate--
let's go high[er]

feeling kinda hungry?
come
down...

cup of tea,
you said i was
quite the...

oh.
what a day.

19.

how far do poems reach?
could you say you still felt my prose
through the confusion of time?

--and if for instance, you stumbled into Love,
might you be able to recall Me?
...on the edges of midnight would you?

--wait for me?
…at the strike of a clock,
would you Break for me?::
rejoice in the mid-day[mess]
of me?

::a girl turned woman by
the turn of calendar pages—

Vilate.

pray for her mother's only daughter.
for her afflictions and addiction to the
feel
of god.

vivrant.
--sunshine.
Shine.
Vivrant.
Looking like--
Sound
i hear you.
i feel you--
i mean...
you know?
yes you-//
...vivrant--
of the quality of vibration,
mispronouced.
the ghetto way
so
it's right...
like that-//

--Bright...

20.

my shit set in stone like
heiroglyphs.
cryptic.

resurrect me through these pages.

& some place between my heart and my mind
control got caught up--
even deep down i couldn't budge
change it up...
i can't love you.

not how either of us wants me to.

i'm black and blue.
i'm a walking tattoo--

i don't trust myself//
how is it i should trust you?

muscle memory getting in tune//
my life been the rubber,
my heart the glue...

...physically...
the thought pains me to move--

my heart been the rubber
your love
been the glue--
i'm the pain of tattoo--

i'm black
&
can't help but leave you blue.

21.

...we could be potent//
--if we got out of the way--
...too much blurred lines
and we already can't see
beyond the bottoms of these
glasses--

blind...//i try to stay
far as possible--
without forgetting how your
fingertips feel...
--we should have ended
our distance a while ago.
maybe we are both enticed by our
own imaginations//.

//the same ones saying
we could exist…
--somewhere far away…
far enuf for you to discard routine…

but right here…
--that love shit you spit made me
fall—
Right back out of it//
cause the shit was beautiful.

and all about another lover.

21.1

//and some times i am ashamed to
say that i loved you…
and allowed you to use me up—
to say that you'd emptied me…
--left me barren—
it disturbs me to say that
you still dwell in the corners of my
soul---

//i often wonder if you are the
boogey man they had
warned me about…
--sleepless nights, tossing and turning
just
Hoping
you might
reach from behind the darkness…

22.

is god that far away?//
        --or nah?

…something tell me we more in proximity
--than we been thinking.//

::we had enrolled in collige.
/the remnants of Rage/

after class was the after party—
//we called on Spirits
        --and danced until the paint lifted off the
        walls.

(twerk twerk twerk)

--queens' bodies possessed://
…libations as we get nearer to
Heaven.

((bounce that ass))
--we remember our conception—

23.

I favor the who of you.
…and besides the hue of you—
it's the only thing that's got my
//mind//
Contorted.
--flame—
…past coals letting your spark
Engulf
History--

…i don't want to own you--
…just wanna see from here//
You//Living.
Your life.
and loving me along the way...
//sporadically if we must//
--hi//
…just not all at once because the Flame
Might burn too bright.

now wouldn't that be
some
thing?

24.

we had…
Made the whole world mad—
what we had
Did
Then…
That time—

Remember?::

...let me play with your
Mind.
--put these words on your
Skin--
bring worlds tumbling
down.
//stimulate your thoughts
and bury into those things
wished upon by your heart...//

...baby take your toes from that cliff.
love is a skydive.

--faith the parachute.
caught on winds brought from far East::
warm and glowing//
like the
flame
we is.

25.

--it's cold outside.
…and creeping through the
Cracks
in these Windows…
//you can't see through though…
can you, Love?

…i want you all the time...
you enjoy me in your leisure--

--and it's cruel that i make myself so
far...

25.1

running..hiding from feeling.
why do we//
(Play this game?)
...indulging in the intrigue of
Addiction...
::i love you::
--and it's too complicated
to be that simple.

...
//despite the magnetism of
you...
i must retreat.

november 1.

to love—to be loved in return…you said you weren't sure if you loved me; my heart took no shock or surprise—it has been without pulse. i tried to love you. i thought it was okay. how do you make tears once a heart has grown cold? this is the ultimate confusion…i thought i was hurting you, but your tie is still on my neck. i am cut off from oxygen, only smoke in my lungs. i didn't want forever, but … i thought the love was real. you didn't know. i don't want to know –it wasn't.

--why do i seek you still though? knowing full well that love is blind, and in order to find//it//i've got to cover my eyes—let it snatch me up by surprise…the movies don't make it seem that way, i reached for you, you pulled away. i was hurt. and they say that's what the truth do to you. …and i let you keep it Real with me, until the lies stopped.

so this letter is as testament. to the longing of reciprocation the artist feels as a result of the cages—placed upon her…by muses come and gone…

letter for halloween scares.

this has to be a trick…[surely it's no treat]—
i'm lost
        why you have to hurt me like that?
        i made you my only.
        was ready to tell the world—
        that you—
        moved me.

-/made my ice cold puddles to splash in/
        beneath the sun//
don't want to be without you.

i hate you, because i love you.
i don't want anyone else.

you became my poem in motion.
i stopped writing.
i breathed you.

every word a poem—
how you filled me//

                you don't
                see
                      you did that/how
                      not?//my heart outside myself—it beat   onto everything
                                                ^
                                    and bled
                                            including you.

continued.

my ink replaced your tears. don't deny my pen—
it writes of you…to you…for you…

      what is love to a heart with holes?
             -a golf ball..playing the course/
             waiting for a (w)hole in 9—

my eyes won't close for the fear of you(r)
        words haunting me—i held everything
        in my hands, no longer guarded//

used to cry in darkness,
        we cut our lights on in the same room.

i am roped down to a wall now—a painting…
nails through my ankles and palms—crucified
        by a Love afraid to let love.

i was angry at myself—if i'd held you tighter…
kissed you twice before walking out the door…
maybe we could have just seen…
        time stretch lazily across the horizon….

more.

i still need you.

and/i still/need you.

don't make me believe and tell me it was a mirage…/i know the love was hot/but baby it never was a desert./until we deserted it.

these poems can't reach that place in you—
that place that will rock you—when you're…
still
these words aren't moving you….
why?

these tears are screaming//

      don't leave! don't tell me this was a lie!

these tears are whispering//

      …don't leave…don't tell me this was a lie…

writing 4 pages worth of poems
writing 4 pages worth of poems

doesn't replace you…doesn't bring the joy in your voice—
the one i could have sworn i just
heard…

didn't i hear it? in your voice…didn't i?

in conclusion.

i heard you smile and i heard your pain go somewhere far…not away…but back…

i was brought to trust you.

let's build.

i'm asking you to feel.

twenty-six.

i left love sleeping as it was when i arrived.
...because true love lets be what is...
//without boundary or constraint..
and i loved you as you were when
i ran into you first...
still...

--so shape shifting you would be an
unecessary evil—

i'd rather love what i can't have..
--and it all stay a reality untouched--

...something about aged wine.

and the Patience in the unknowns
of the chambers where it is kept...

--out of sight,
nowhere near out of mind.

www.ingramcontent.com/pod-product-compliance
Lightning Source LLC
Chambersburg PA
CBHW050912180526
45159CB00007B/2887